Steps to Overcome Addiction

A Comprehensive Guide to Reclaiming Your Life

By

Evaristus Chukwugoziem Okonkwo

Obasi Reloaded Publishing Inc.

ISBN: 9798859022908

Imprint: Independently published

First Edition: 2023

Printed in the United States of America.

Cover design by Oko Obasi

CONTENTS

Introduction

- Introduce the prevalence and impact of addiction on individuals and society.

- Highlight the importance of seeking help and taking proactive steps towards recovery.

Chapter 1: Understanding Addiction

- Define addiction and explain its various forms (substance, behavioral, etc.).

Chapter 2: Discuss the science behind addiction, including its effects on the brain and neurotransmitters.

Chapter 3: Acceptance and Self-Reflection

- Encourage readers to acknowledge their addiction and the consequences it has brought.

- Guide readers through self-reflection exercises to understand the triggers, emotions, and patterns associated with their addiction.......9

Chapter 4: Seeking Professional Help

- Stress the importance of consulting healthcare professionals, therapists, and counselors.

- Detail the types of professionals available and their roles in the recovery process.

- Provide tips for finding the right treatment program or therapist.

Chapter 5: Setting Recovery Goals

- Discuss the significance of setting clear and achievable goals for recovery.

- Walk readers through the process of defining short-term and long-term goals related to quitting their addiction.

Chapter 6: Building a Supportive Network

- Highlight the role of friends, family, and support groups in the recovery journey.

- Offer advice on how to communicate with loved ones about the addiction and request their support.

Chapter 7: Creating Healthy Habits

- Provide guidance on establishing a daily routine that includes exercise, nutrition, and sleep.

- Explain how a healthy lifestyle can positively impact mental and physical well-being during recovery.

Chapter 8: Coping Mechanisms and Stress Management

- Explore various coping strategies to manage stress, anxiety, and cravings.

- Include mindfulness techniques, meditation, deep breathing exercises, and creative outlets.

Chapter 9: Breaking Triggers and Patterns

- Help readers identify triggers, situations, and environments that contribute to their addictive behavior.

- Offer strategies to avoid or navigate these triggers and replace negative habits with positive alternatives.

Chapter 10: Understanding Relapse and Resilience

- Explain that relapses can be a natural part of the recovery process and shouldn't be seen as failure.

- Provide insights on how to learn from relapses, strengthen resilience, and continue moving forward.

Chapter 11: Embracing New Beginnings

- Discuss the transformation that occurs during the recovery journey.

- Offer guidance on maintaining sobriety, enjoying life without addiction, and pursuing personal growth.

Chapter 12: Inspiring Recovery Stories

- Share real-life recovery stories to motivate and inspire readers.

- Showcase diverse experiences of overcoming different types of addictions and challenges.

Chapter 13: Resources and Next Steps

- Compile a list of resources, websites, helplines, and organizations that offer support for addiction recovery.

- Provide guidance on how to continue seeking help, staying accountable, and maintaining progress.

Conclusion

- Summarize the key takeaways from the book.

- Reinforce the message of hope, resilience, and the possibility of a brighter future after overcoming addiction.

Reference

About the Author

Dedication

This book is dedicated to the memory of my late parents, the pillars of my foundation—Mr. Martin Okonkwo and Mrs. Evangeline Okonkwo. Their unwavering love and teachings continue to resonate within me. Also to my dearly departed brother—Mr. Obinwanne Okonkwo, whose memory lives on.

ACKNOWLEDGEMENT

In moments of reflection and gratitude, I am privileged to acknowledge individuals who have stood as pillars of unwavering support and inspiration.

First and foremost I humbly acknowledge the benevolence of Almighty GOD, whose guidance and blessings have illuminated my path.

Hon. Amala Anazodo, your presence has been a beacon of encouragement, guiding me with your wisdom and guidance.

Dr. Ifejika, your contributions have enriched my path with knowledge and insight, and for that, I am profoundly grateful.

Attorney Ngozi Okonkwo, your expertise and dedication have illuminated my way, and I extend my heartfelt appreciation.

A special tribute to my big brother, Obika Okonkwo—your guidance, mentorship, and sibling bond have been a source of strength that words cannot fully convey., Also my other siblings Very Rev Fr.Kyrian Kenechukwu Okonkwo, a guiding light in faith—I offer my enduring respect. My beloved sister Dr. Chioma Maryjane Okonkwo, your support and wisdom have been invaluable, and for that, I am deeply grateful.

I extend my heartfelt appreciation to Mr. and Mrs. Azubuike Edward Okechie for nurturing and raising an extraordinary daughter who has become my cherished wife. Your love, values, and guidance have played a pivotal role in shaping the remarkable person she is today, and I am truly grateful for the gift of her presence in my life. Your influence shines brightly in her character, and I am honored to be a part of your wonderful family.

In the tapestry of my life, my beloved wife, Mrs. Chinenye Juliet Okonkwo, stands as my rock. Your presence is my sanctuary, and your partnership, my strength.

My children, Isioma Chukwummeri Okonkwo and Evaristus Chukwugozirim Okonkwo, you are the embodiment of my hopes and dreams. Your existence fuels my aspirations.

To my brother and friend Dr.Oko Obasi I thank you for pointing me in this direction. I very much appreciate you. Finally to each person who has touched my journey, imparting wisdom, offering solace, and igniting inspiration, I extend my sincerest gratitude.

With humility and reverence, I recognize that my path is adorned with the love, support, and teachings of these remarkable souls. May their legacies continue to guide and shape my voyage through life.

EVARISTUS CHUKWUGOZIEM OKONKWO

STEPS TO OVERCOME ADDICTION

A Comprehensive Guide to Reclaiming Your Life

PREFACE: A JOURNEY TOWARDS FREEDOM

In a world where addiction can cast a shadow over even the brightest of lives, this book serves as a guiding light—a beacon of hope for those seeking to break free from the chains of dependency. It is a roadmap for individuals who have made the courageous decision to confront their addiction head-on and embark on a transformative journey towards recovery.

Addiction is a formidable adversary, capable of ensnaring the mind, body, and spirit. It's a battle that's often fought in silence, yet its impact ripples through families, friendships, and communities. This book is born out of the belief that no one should have to face this battle alone. It is a testament to the resilience of the human spirit, showcasing the strength that emerges when individuals dare to reclaim their lives from addiction's grip.

Throughout the pages of this book, you will find a comprehensive framework—a collection of insights, strategies, and stories—crafted to empower you along your path to recovery. From understanding the intricacies of addiction's hold on the brain to building a robust support system, from cultivating healthy habits to navigating the bumps in the road, each chapter is a stepping stone on your journey towards healing and transformation.

As you delve into the stories of those who have overcome addiction, remember that their journeys are a testament to the indomitable spirit within us all. Each chapter is an opportunity for reflection, self-discovery, and growth. The path won't always be smooth, and setbacks may occur, but the journey is marked by progress, triumphs, and the renewal of purpose.

This book is a reminder that seeking help is not a sign of weakness, but rather a courageous act of self-love. It's an acknowledgment that there is strength in vulnerability, and that healing begins when you choose to share your burdens with those who care. Whether you are navigating addiction yourself or supporting someone on this journey, know that you are not alone. The path to recovery is paved with compassion, understanding, and a willingness to embrace change.

May this book serve as a source of inspiration, education, and empowerment. May it be a companion on your journey—a friend that offers guidance when the road gets tough and celebrates every victory, no matter how small. You have within you the power to overcome, to transform, and to step into a brighter, addiction-free future. Your journey starts now, and this book is here to light the way.

With unwavering support,

Evaristus Chukwugoziem Okonkwo

Nnewi, Anambra State

Nigeria

CHAPTER 1

UNDERSTANDING ADDICTION

"Recognize your value, for it's the first step towards breaking free."

Defining Addiction: Unraveling the Chains

Addiction is a word that carries both weight and mystery. It's a force that has touched millions of lives, weaving a web of challenges that extend beyond the individual to encompass families, communities, and societies at large. But what is addiction, truly? How does it manifest, and why does it persist? In this chapter, we'll delve into the heart of addiction, exploring its various forms, the science that underpins it, and dispelling some of the myths that shroud it in misunderstanding.

Deciphering the Complexity of Addiction

The labyrinthine realm of addiction defies a single definition, its contours shifting with the nuances of perception. According to the venerable Oxford Dictionary, addiction manifests as "the fact or condition of being addicted to a particular substance or activity". Merriam-Webster, too, proffers a perspective, encapsulating addiction as "a compulsive, chronic, physiological or psychological need for a habit-forming substance, behavior, or activity having harmful physical, psychological, or social effects and typically causing well-defined symptoms (such as anxiety, irritability, tremors, or nausea) upon withdrawal or abstinence". And Healthline, delving into the depths of neurological intricacies, describes addiction as "a chronic dysfunction of the brain system that involves reward, motivation, and memory. It's about the way your body craves a substance or behavior, especially if it causes a compulsive or obsessive pursuit of 'reward' and lack of concern over consequences".

Forms of Addiction: Beyond the Obvious

When we hear the word "addiction," our minds often jump to substances like drugs and alcohol. However, addiction is a multifaceted phenomenon that extends beyond the realm of substances. Behavioural addictions—such as gambling, internet use, shopping, and even certain eating behaviours—also fall under its umbrella. These behavioural addictions are driven by similar mechanisms in the brain, where the pursuit of a reward becomes compulsive and negatively impacts one's life.

There are various types of addiction that individuals can experience. These include:

1. Substance Addictions:

   - Alcohol addiction

   - Drug addiction (e.g., opioids, cocaine, methamphetamine)

   - Tobacco addiction (nicotine)

2. Behavioral Addictions:

   - Gambling addiction

   - Internet gaming disorder

   - Shopping addiction

   - Food addiction

   - Sex addiction

   - Work addiction

3. Process Addictions:

   - Compulsive gambling

   - Compulsive spending

   - Compulsive eating

   - Compulsive sexual behavior

4. Technology Addictions:

   - Internet addiction

   - Social media addiction

5. Risk-Taking Addictions:

   - Thrill-seeking addiction

   - Extreme sports addiction

6. Love and Relationship Addictions:

   - Love addiction

   - Codependency

7. Exercise Addiction:

   - Compulsive exercise

8. Prescription Medication Addictions:

   - Opioid painkiller addiction

   - Benzodiazepine addiction

9. Video Game Addiction:

   - Excessive video gaming

10. Workaholism:

   - Obsessive work addiction

It's important to note that these types of addiction can have varying degrees of impact on individuals' lives and may require different approaches to treatment and recovery.

Not a respecter of persons: affects all ages

Addiction presents itself as an intricate and multi-dimensional phenomenon, impacting individuals of diverse ages, backgrounds, and circumstances. As outlined in the World Drug Report 2019, an astonishing 35 million individuals globally grapple with drug use disorders, necessitating treatment services[1]. Remarkably, merely one in seven of these individuals receive the necessary treatment they require[2]. The pervasiveness, nuances, and consequences of addiction differ amongst age groups, just as the factors influencing the initiation, perpetuation, and cessation of substance use.

Among these age groups, young adults between 18 and 25 exhibit notably higher rates of addiction. This demographic often engages in experimentation with a spectrum of substances, including alcohol, cannabis, cocaine, heroin, and synthetic drugs. Compounded by peer pressure, societal norms, and environmental triggers, their vulnerability to drug use and reinforcement increases[1]. It is not uncommon for many young adults to postpone addressing their addiction until their 30s or 40s, potentially negatively impacting their holistic well-being – mentally, physically, and socially.

Conversely, older adults aged 65 and above encounter distinct challenges linked to addiction. This group tends to grapple with chronic pain, insomnia, anxiety, depression, and other medical conditions that could necessitate prescription drugs[1]. Yet, certain prescription drugs, such as opioids and benzodiazepines, carry a substantial risk of abuse and dependency. Older adults might resort to misusing alcohol or illicit substances as a response to feelings of loneliness, sorrow, or monotony[1]. Due to factors like diminished tolerance, slower metabolism, and multiple coexisting health conditions, the ramifications of addiction among older adults are often more severe and perilous.

It is evident that addiction doesn't subscribe to a uniform mold. Instead, it mandates a comprehensive and tailored strategy that takes into consideration the unique requisites and attributes of varying age groups. The design of preventative and therapeutic measures should be grounded in evidence-based methodologies, addressing the biological, psychological, social, and environmental elements that influence substance use and addiction.

Furthermore, it is crucial to acknowledge addiction as a persistent and recurring ailment necessitating extended care and encouragement. By understanding the intricate array of addiction experiences across different age brackets, we can provide more effective support to those grappling with this challenge, facilitating their journey towards recovery and healthier lives.

CHAPTER 2

EXPLORING ADDICTION

**"Addiction doesn't define your worth;
your journey to recovery does."**

A Dichotomy of Chemical and Behavioural

Within the intricate nature of addiction, two distinct threads emerge: Chemical Addiction and Behavioural Addiction. Each thread weaves a narrative that captures the essence of compulsive allure and unyielding behaviours, manifesting in different ways.

Chemical Addiction: Binding Ties to Substances

Chemical addiction unfurls its grip through the consumption of substances that ensnare the senses. A tumultuous relationship forms, driven by the relentless pursuit of intoxication, even in the face of dire consequences. This category spans an array of substances, from the legal to the illicit:

- Alcohol: An age-old intoxicant that clouds judgment and distorts reality.

- Tobacco: A pervasive habit, entwined with nicotine's grasp.

- Opioids: The potent embrace of heroin and prescription drugs that numb pain and awareness.

- Cocaine: A stimulant that surges euphoria, followed by the cruel descent into craving.

- Cannabis: The most commonly used illegal drug globally, whispered by various names.

- Amphetamines: A realm of stimulants, including the notorious methamphetamines.

Behavioural Addiction: Compulsive Pursuits

The behavioural counterpart to chemical addiction, behavioural addiction, thrives in the realm of compulsive behaviours that offer no true benefit. It's the siren call of actions that persist, despite reason and consequence:

- Gambling: The thrill of risk, capturing hearts and fortunes alike.

- Shopping: A consuming pursuit, masking emotional needs in material acquisition.

- Sex: A primal drive that spirals into obsession and compulsivity.

The Cannabis Conundrum: A Global Phenomenon

Cannabis, a name echoing across continents, stands as the most commonly used illegal drug worldwide. It seizes half of all drug seizures on a global scale, traversing borders, cultures, and societies. According to the World Health Organization (WHO), approximately 147 million people, constituting 2.5% of the world's population, indulge in cannabis annually—a prevalence far surpassing cocaine and opiates.

In the shadow of these staggering numbers, a troubling reality emerges. The year 2018 bore witness to almost 270 million illegal drug users worldwide, of whom 35.6 million bore the mark of "problem drug users." This ominous category encompassed those entangled in drug use disorders, bearing witness to the harrowing grip of addiction's clutches.

As the threads of chemical and behavioural addiction continue to weave through the fabric of human experience, societies grapple with understanding, intervention, and support. In this dance between allure and adversity, a collective journey unfolds—a journey towards comprehending the labyrinthine nature of addiction and forging pathways to liberation.

Unravelling the Roots of Addiction

The origins of addiction lie in an intricate interplay between the physical and psychological, giving rise to a tantalizing "high" that tightens its grip over time. This escalating pursuit leads to prolonged usage of substances or engagement in behaviours, all in the quest to rekindle the same euphoric sensation. With every step, the battle to break free becomes an uphill struggle.

The Brain's Role: A Neurochemical Dance

At the heart of addiction lies the intricate dance of neurochemicals within the brain. It's a story of pleasure, reinforcement, and sometimes, a hijacking of the brain's reward system. Central to this system is dopamine—a neurotransmitter that signals pleasure and motivation. When we engage in pleasurable activities, like eating, socializing, or using substances, our brain releases dopamine. Over time, with repeated exposure to substances or behaviors that flood the brain with dopamine, changes occur in the brain's structure and function.

The Neurotransmitter Tug-of-War

The brain adapts to this heightened dopamine activity by reducing its sensitivity to the neurotransmitter. As a result, individuals may find that they need larger amounts of the substance or behavior to achieve the same pleasurable effect—a phenomenon known as tolerance. Additionally, the brain's reward system becomes dysregulated, leading to cravings, withdrawal symptoms, and an overpowering urge to engage in the addictive behavior.

The Brain's Influence

The enigmatic realm of addiction hinges on the brain's intricate workings. While some may dabble in a substance or behavior and move on, others find themselves ensnared in addiction's clutches. The frontal lobes of the brain, gatekeepers of delayed gratification, play a pivotal role. However, in addiction, the once-disciplined frontal lobe falters, bestowing immediate gratification.

Other brain domains, including the anterior cingulate cortex and the nucleus accumbens—a hub of pleasure—also come into play. When exposed to addictive stimuli, their response amplifies, magnifying the allure.

Underlying causes, like chemical imbalances and mental disorders such as schizophrenia or bipolar disorder, cast their shadow. These afflictions breed coping mechanisms that metamorphose into addictions, intertwining the strands of mental health and addiction.

The Early Imprint

Experts posit that the seeds of addiction are often sown through early, repetitive encounters with addictive elements. Genetics, too, exert influence—upping addiction's odds by 50%, notes the American Society of Addiction Medicine. Yet, familial predisposition is not an absolute sentence.

The stage is further set by environment and culture. These factors choreograph how an individual responds to a substance or behavior. The absence or disruption of a social support system can steer one toward addictive paths. Trauma, a formidable force, can disrupt coping mechanisms and thrust individuals into the realm of addictive behaviors.

Stages of Addiction

The saga of addiction is a multi-act drama, each stage marked by distinct shifts in brain and body dynamics:

1. Experimentation: The curious phase, where one ventures into substance use or behaviors.

2. Social or Regular: Transitioning to social usage, seeking camaraderie or acceptance.

3. Problem or Risk: The perilous pivot, where recklessness defies consequences.

4. Dependency: The pinnacle, where daily or repeated engagement prevails, despite potential fallout.

As the narrative unfolds, addiction's labyrinthine grip deepens, sculpting paths through curiosity, camaraderie, recklessness, and relentless need. In this intricate dance between allure and adversity, understanding the multifaceted underpinnings of addiction paves the way toward compassionate intervention and healing.

Unraveling the Fabric of Addiction

So, what is addiction at its core? It emerges as a chronic, ceaseless condition, manifesting as an unrelenting urge to seek and partake in a substance or activity, even in the face of detrimental repercussions. Its impact extends beyond individual boundaries, reverberating through health, relationships, and life's very essence. The imperative to seek help at the inception of addictive signs is paramount, a lifeline that can mitigate the depths of addiction's entanglements.

The Disease Within: Embracing a Paradigm Shift

Indeed, addiction is not merely a series of unfortunate decisions, nor a deficiency of willpower. It stands as a disease, an unyielding chronic condition etched into the annals of the mind. As ratified by the American Society of Addiction Medicine (ASAM), addiction is a disorder rooted in the very synapses of the brain—a departure from equilibrium, a shift in brain chemistry that transcends individual volition.

Diverse Avenues of Addiction: A Dual Realm

The landscape of addiction unfurls into two distinct territories: substance addictions and non-substance addictions. Healthcare now terms substance addiction as substance use disorder, a facet embedded within the realm of the Diagnostic and Statistical Manual of Mental Disorders (DSM-5). This encompassing umbrella includes a myriad of substances, from alcohol and nicotine to opioids and stimulants, each ensnaring the reward centers of the brain with intoxicating allure.

The Enigma of Behavioral Addiction: A Limited Spectrum

Behavioral addictions, a domain currently explored with measured caution, envelop activities capable of eliciting the brain's reward mechanism. Gambling disorder stands as the lone entrant in the DSM-5's roster of diagnosable behavioral addictions. Nonetheless, the domain of behavioral addictions extends beyond, enveloping activities from eating and shopping to video gaming and internet usage. A universe teeming with compulsive pursuits that, while not universally recognized, share the potential to disrupt and debilitate lives.

Process addictions, also known as behavioral addictions, involve engaging in repetitive behaviors or activities that provide pleasure or relief but can lead to negative consequences over time. Unlike substance addictions that involve the consumption of a specific substance, process addictions center around certain behaviors. Some common process addictions include:

1. Compulsive Gambling:

Compulsive gambling, also known as gambling addiction or gambling disorder, is characterized by an inability to control the urge to gamble despite negative consequences. People with this addiction may experience intense cravings to gamble, spend excessive amounts of money on gambling activities, and become preoccupied with gambling-related thoughts. The addiction can lead to financial problems, strained relationships, and even legal issues.

2. Compulsive Spending:

Compulsive spending, also referred to as shopping addiction or compulsive buying disorder, involves an uncontrollable urge to shop and spend money, often resulting in financial distress. People with this addiction may shop to alleviate negative emotions, seek excitement, or achieve a sense of control. Compulsive spending can lead to debt, financial instability, and feelings of guilt or shame.

3. Compulsive Eating:

Compulsive eating, also known as binge eating disorder, is characterized by recurrent episodes of consuming large amounts of food in a short period, often accompanied by feelings of lack of control and guilt. Individuals with this addiction may use food to cope with emotions, stress, or boredom. Compulsive eating can lead to obesity, physical health issues, and psychological distress.

4. Compulsive Sexual Behavior:

Compulsive sexual behavior, sometimes referred to as hypersexual disorder or sex addiction, involves an intense preoccupation with sexual thoughts, fantasies, and behaviors.

People with this addiction may engage in excessive sexual activities, seek out multiple partners, and have difficulty controlling their sexual impulses. Compulsive sexual behavior can lead to relationship problems, social isolation, and a decreased quality of life.

Process addictions share common characteristics with substance addictions, such as an inability to control the behavior, withdrawal symptoms when the behavior is not engaged in, and negative impacts on various aspects of life. These addictions are often driven by psychological and emotional factors, such as seeking pleasure, relief from stress, or a way to cope with underlying issues.

Treatment for process addictions typically involves therapy, counseling, support groups, and behavioral interventions. Cognitive-behavioral therapy (CBT), dialectical behavior therapy (DBT), and motivational interviewing are commonly used approaches to address the underlying causes of the addiction and develop healthier coping strategies.

It's important to recognize that process addictions can have a significant impact on an individual's overall well-being and functioning. Seeking professional help and support is crucial for managing and overcoming these types of addictions.

Risk-taking addictions involve seeking out activities or behaviors that provide an adrenaline rush, excitement, or a sense of danger. These addictions are characterized by engaging in activities that carry a significant level of risk, often leading to physical harm, injury, or life-threatening situations. Two common risk-taking addictions are thrill-seeking addiction and extreme sports addiction:

1. Thrill-Seeking Addiction:

Thrill-seeking addiction refers to the compulsive pursuit of novel and intense experiences that trigger adrenaline and excitement. Individuals with this addiction may constantly seek out risky situations or engage in impulsive behaviors to experience the rush associated with adrenaline. Examples include reckless driving, participating in dangerous stunts, or engaging in risky sexual behaviors.

Thrill-seeking addiction can have serious consequences, including accidents, injuries, and legal troubles.

2. Extreme Sports Addiction:

Extreme sports addiction involves an obsessive need to participate in high-risk and adrenaline-pumping sports and activities. These activities often push the limits of physical and mental endurance, such as skydiving, BASE jumping, snowboarding in extreme conditions, and rock climbing at dangerous heights. While extreme sports can provide a sense of accomplishment and excitement, individuals with an extreme sports addiction may engage in these activities excessively and compulsively, often disregarding safety precautions.

Risk-taking addictions are driven by a combination of factors, including the desire for novelty, the need for stimulation, and the thrill of defying danger. These addictions can lead to a range of negative outcomes, including physical injuries, psychological distress, strained relationships, and a negative impact on overall well-being.

Treatment for risk-taking addictions involves addressing the underlying psychological and emotional factors that contribute to the addiction. Cognitive-behavioral therapy (CBT) and counseling can help individuals develop healthier coping mechanisms, improve risk assessment skills, and enhance decision-making abilities. It's important for individuals with risk-taking addictions to learn to balance their desire for excitement with responsible behavior and safety precautions.

Prevention is also crucial, and education about the potential dangers of risky behaviors and the importance of making informed choices can help reduce the likelihood of developing risk-taking addictions. Additionally, engaging in alternative activities that provide a sense of adventure and excitement while minimizing the risk of harm can be a constructive way to channel the desire for thrill-seeking behaviors.

Love and Relationship Addictions:

Love and relationship addictions are characterized by an unhealthy and compulsive dependence on romantic relationships and the intense emotional experiences associated with them. Individuals with these types of addictions often prioritize their relationships to an extent that it becomes detrimental to their well-being. Three common love and relationship addictions are love addiction, codependency, and exercise addiction:

1. Love Addiction:

Love addiction, also known as obsessive love disorder, refers to an intense preoccupation with being in a romantic relationship. Individuals with love addiction may constantly seek out new relationships, become infatuated with partners, and experience extreme emotional highs and lows. They may feel incomplete or anxious when not in a relationship, leading them to rush into new relationships without fully considering compatibility. This addiction can result in a cycle of short-lived and intense relationships.

2. Codependency:

Codependency involves an unhealthy and one-sided reliance on a partner or relationship for emotional well-being.

People with codependency often prioritize their partner's needs and feelings over their own, neglecting their own self-care and boundaries. They may struggle to express their own emotions and rely on their partner for validation and a sense of identity. Codependent relationships can become enmeshed and toxic, leading to emotional distress for both individuals.

3. Exercise Addiction:

While not directly related to romantic relationships, exercise addiction is another form of addictive behavior that can impact relationships. Exercise addiction involves an excessive and compulsive need to engage in physical activity, often driven by the pursuit of an ideal body image or a sense of control. Individuals with exercise addiction may prioritize workouts over spending time with loved ones, leading to strained relationships and isolation. The addiction can also negatively affect physical health if taken to extremes.

Addressing love and relationship addictions often requires a combination of therapy, counseling, and support. Cognitive-behavioral therapy (CBT) can help individuals recognize and challenge unhealthy patterns of thinking and behavior. Additionally, couples therapy or family therapy may be beneficial for those in codependent relationships, helping both parties establish healthy boundaries and improve communication.

For exercise addiction, it's important to seek guidance from healthcare professionals who can provide balanced exercise recommendations and monitor physical health. Developing a healthy relationship with exercise involves finding a balance between physical activity and other aspects of life, including relationships and personal well-being.

Overall, addressing love and relationship addictions requires a commitment to personal growth, self-awareness, and building healthy connections with oneself and others. It's important to remember that seeking help and support is a sign of strength and a step toward breaking free from unhealthy patterns.

Forefront of Addiction: The Sobering Truth

Alcohol use disorder stands as a prevailing force in the realm of substance addictions, with nicotine and marijuana trailing in its wake. A staggering 10% of individuals aged 12 or older in the United States bear the mantle of alcohol use disorder—an evocative testament to addiction's reach. A study carried out in Ibadan, Nigeria, shed light on the prevalence of potential Alcohol Use Disorder (AUD) among individuals consuming alcohol in open public spaces.

The findings revealed a notable prevalence rate of 39.5%. Interestingly, the study also uncovered that adherence to the Islamic faith acted as a deterrent against potential AUD. Conversely, residence in rural areas and engagement in cigarette smoking were identified as predictors of potential AUD. However, it's essential to acknowledge the study's limitations—it specifically focused on outdoor drinkers in public areas, and therefore might not offer a comprehensive representation of Nigeria's entire population.

In the quest to decipher addiction's enigma, the manifestations are as varied as the individuals they inhabit. Symptoms encompass the inability to cease, a mounting tolerance, a relentless focus, loss of control, and the shadow of withdrawal. The genesis of addiction is complex, merging genetics, mental health conditions, and environmental factors in a unique, intricate alchemy.

Dispelling Misconceptions: Clearing the Fog

Misconceptions about addiction can hinder both understanding and compassion. One common misconception is that addiction is purely a matter of willpower—that individuals could stop if they tried hard enough. In reality, addiction is a complex interplay of genetic, environmental, and neurological factors. It's not a moral failing, but a medical condition that requires comprehensive treatment and support.

The Road Ahead: Knowledge as Empowerment

Understanding addiction is the first step towards recovery—for individuals and for society. By recognizing the scientific underpinnings of addiction, we can shift our perspectives from blame to empathy. We can appreciate that addiction is not a flaw of character, but a challenge that demands a holistic approach encompassing medical intervention, therapy, social support, and a deep commitment to change.

In the following chapters, we will explore the journey of recovery. We will delve into the strategies that empower individuals to break free from addiction's grasp, building a foundation for a healthier and more fulfilling life. Remember, knowledge is the cornerstone of change, and as we arm ourselves with understanding, we take a decisive step towards a brighter, addiction-free future.

In our quest to understand addiction, we illuminate its darkened corners, paving the way for empathy, support, and intervention. As we continue this exploration, remember that knowledge is not merely a beacon—it's a lifeline.

CHAPTER 3

ACCEPTANCE AND SELF-REFLECTION

Your worthiness transcends the chains of addiction.

In the intricate journey of overcoming addiction, a pivotal juncture emerges: the crossroads of acceptance and self-reflection. This chapter delves into the profound significance of acknowledging one's addiction and embarking on a voyage of self-discovery.

Embracing Acceptance and Embarking on Self-Reflection in Addiction Recovery

Within the realm of addiction recovery, two guiding stars illuminate the path to transformation: Acceptance and self-reflection. These pillars, each with its unique essence, converge to create a transformative journey towards healing and growth.

Acceptance: Illuminating Reality

At the heart of the recovery journey lies the pivotal act of acceptance—a deliberate embrace of one's reality. This profound process involves facing the truth of one's addiction head-on, acknowledging its presence, and embracing the impact it has had on life's tapestry[1]. With acceptance, the veil of denial is lifted, paving the way for a candid examination of one's actions and choices.

Empowerment through Responsibility: Acceptance entails not only recognizing the consequences of addiction but also taking ownership of one's role in the journey. It's a stepping stone towards accountability and a testament to the courage to confront the shadows of the past.

Self-Reflection: A Gaze Inward

Complementary to acceptance is self-reflection—a journey inward to explore the intricate landscape of thoughts, emotions, and behaviors. This introspective process invites individuals to traverse the labyrinth of their inner world, fostering a deeper understanding of themselves[2].

Unveiling the Layers: Self-reflection empowers individuals to peel back the layers of their psyche, unveiling the motivations and triggers that once fueled addictive patterns. This illumination casts light on the emotional undercurrents that might have remained hidden.

From Insight to Transformation: Armed with insights gained through self-reflection, individuals are equipped to chart a new course. The recognition of patterns, vulnerabilities, and emotional dynamics paves the way for the cultivation of healthier coping mechanisms and transformative change.

A Tapestry of Healing

Acceptance and self-reflection intertwine in the fabric of recovery, stitching together a narrative of growth and transformation. As individuals practice acceptance, the shackles of self-blame and judgment are released, making space for positive change and personal evolution. This practice also nurtures emotional intelligence and resilience, forging a sturdy armor to face the hurdles of recovery.

Self-reflection, on the other hand, delves beneath the surface, uncovering the roots of addiction and deciphering the complexities of one's journey. This self-discovery forms the bedrock upon which new habits, responses, and perspectives are built.

In conclusion, acceptance and self-reflection are twin beacons in the expedition of addiction recovery. Through acceptance, the path to healing is paved with honesty and accountability. Self-reflection, a journey within, offers invaluable insights that guide the transformation from within. Together, these pillars illuminate a path of healing, growth, and self-discovery—a journey not merely of recovery, but of becoming.

Embracing the Truth: Acknowledging Addiction's Hold

Before the dawn of transformation can break through, the shadows of denial must be cast aside. The first step towards liberation is the courageous acknowledgment of one's addiction. It's a profound moment of truth, where the veil of self-deception is lifted, revealing the impact addiction has woven into the fabric of one's life.

Confronting Consequences: This section examines the ripple effects of addiction—how it has seeped into relationships, health, and aspirations. By unearthing these consequences, readers are prompted to confront the stark reality of their journey thus far.

Mirror of the Soul: Self-Reflection Unveiled

With acknowledgment comes the gateway to a journey of self-reflection—an exploration that unearths the why behind the what. This section provides readers with guidance on introspection techniques, guiding them to delve deep within themselves:

Tracing Triggers: Identifying the catalysts that trigger addictive behaviors is a transformative exercise. Through insightful prompts, readers dissect the moments, emotions, and situations that set the wheels of addiction in motion.

Unveiling Emotions: Emotions, often buried beneath layers of pain and habit, play a pivotal role in addiction. This section empowers readers to peel back those layers, unraveling the emotional tapestry that binds them to their addictive cycles.

Patterns and Habits: Habitual patterns, like well-trodden pathways, lead to familiar destinations. Here, readers navigate through the labyrinth of their habits, discerning patterns that perpetuate their addiction. This revelation is a compass that points toward change.

The Canvas of Healing: Crafting a Path Forward

As readers immerse themselves in the waters of self-reflection, they stand at the precipice of healing. This chapter concludes by encouraging readers to synthesize their insights, laying the foundation for transformation:

Constructing a Blueprint: Armed with newfound awareness, readers are poised to craft a personalized blueprint for change. This blueprint, a testament to their commitment, paves the way for a future free from the clutches of addiction.

The Journey Continues: Acknowledgment and self-reflection are not destinations but milestones along the journey. This chapter concludes by reminding readers that this expedition is not solitary—the path to healing is lined with support, resources, and the promise of growth.

In this chapter, readers are beckoned to stand at the crossroads, where acceptance unfurls its wings and self-reflection unfurls its map. It's a chapter that invites them to engage with their truth, confront their shadows, and kindle the flames of change—a journey of profound significance.

CHAPTER 4

SEEKING PROFESSIONAL HELP

"Asking for help is really the beginning of any sort of recovery process."

- Marc Maron

In the labyrinth of addiction recovery, the compass guiding the way is the expertise of healthcare professionals, therapists, and counselors. This chapter unveils the pivotal role of seeking professional help—a transformative step towards healing, growth, and reclaiming one's life.

The Crucial Step: Consulting Professionals

Amidst the challenges of addiction recovery, seeking professional guidance is a beacon of hope. This chapter underscores the importance of this step—a lifeline that navigates individuals towards a comprehensive and structured path to recovery.

Types of Professionals and Their Roles

Within the realm of addiction recovery, a tapestry of professionals is poised to lend their expertise. This section delves into the diverse roles that these professionals play:

Medical Experts: Physicians and addiction medicine specialists assess physical health, withdrawal symptoms, and medical complications. Their expertise guides the detoxification process and ensures the safety of individuals as they embark on recovery.

Therapists and Counselors: These professionals serve as guides through the emotional landscape of recovery. Therapists employ evidence-based techniques to uncover the psychological triggers, traumas, and patterns that underpin addiction. Counselors offer support, coping strategies, and a safe space for reflection.

Psychiatrists: In cases of co-occurring mental health disorders, psychiatrists provide dual expertise in addressing both addiction and mental health. They prescribe medications when necessary and offer comprehensive treatment plans.

Navigating the Selection Process

Choosing the right treatment program or therapist is akin to finding a compass that resonates with one's journey. This section offers practical advice to empower individuals in their search:

Research and Referrals: Research various treatment options and seek referrals from trusted sources, such as healthcare professionals, friends, or support groups. Online resources and reviews can also provide insights.

Assess Credentials: Verify the credentials of professionals or treatment centers. Credentials such as licensure, certifications, and affiliations with reputable organizations ensure quality care.

Tailoring to Individual Needs: Every recovery journey is unique. Seek professionals who offer personalized treatment plans that address individual needs, challenges, and goals.

Interview and Consultation: Consider consultations or interviews with potential therapists or treatment centers. This interaction provides a glimpse into their approach, philosophy, and compatibility with your journey.

A Path Illuminated by Professionals

In the canvas of addiction recovery, the strokes of professionals paint a portrait of transformation. Chapter 3 underscores the significance of seeking their expertise—a testament to the courage to reach out, embrace guidance, and navigate the path to recovery.

Addiction does not discriminate based on age, status, or any other factors.

It is a relentless force that can impact individuals from all walks of life. Whether young or old, rich or poor, addiction can affect anyone, tearing through the fabric of their lives and leaving a trail of destruction in its wake.

One of the most important lessons to understand about addiction is that it is not a respecter of persons. It can infiltrate the lives of the young and impressionable, leading them down a treacherous path before they even realize the gravity of their situation. At the same time, it can ensnare those who have experienced decades of life, catching them off guard and challenging their resilience.

Addiction does not care about one's accomplishments, social status, or educational background. It is blind to the awards on the shelf, the titles held, or the degrees earned. It's a stark reminder that nobody is immune to its grasp. The allure of substances or compulsive behaviors can be potent, luring individuals from all walks of life into its web.

The story of addiction spans across generations, cultures, and social strata. It affects parents, professionals, students, celebrities, and every other individual in between. This truth serves as a powerful equalizer, reminding us that addiction can touch anyone, irrespective of their outward appearances or public personas.

Understanding that addiction does not discriminate is crucial for dispelling misconceptions and judgments. It helps create a compassionate approach toward those who are struggling, emphasizing that anyone can fall victim to its grip. Acknowledging this fact also encourages proactive efforts to prevent addiction, foster awareness, and provide support for those in need.

Ultimately, recognizing that addiction is not a respecter of persons reinforces the importance of empathy, understanding, and open dialogue. It prompts society to come together to address this universal challenge and create a collective response that emphasizes prevention, treatment, and a supportive environment for recovery.

Through the collective wisdom of medical experts, therapists, counselors, and psychiatrists, individuals are empowered to dismantle the chains of addiction and rebuild their lives. In the embrace of professional help, a symphony of healing, growth, and empowerment unfolds—an ode to the profound impact of seeking the right compass on the journey to recovery.

CHAPTER 5

SETTING RECOVERY GOALS

Your journey to recovery is a testament to your inherent worth.

In the symphony of addiction recovery, the power of setting goals orchestrates a harmonious journey towards transformation. This chapter delves into the profound impact of setting clear and achievable goals—a compass that guides individuals through the intricate maze of recovery.

The Pillars of Progress: Setting Recovery Goals

At the core of recovery lies the art of setting goals—a cornerstone that propels individuals towards a future untainted by addiction's grasp. This chapter casts light upon the significance of this practice and unfolds a roadmap for readers to embark upon.

The Power of Purpose: Why Set Goals?

Setting goals in the realm of addiction recovery is akin to sketching a vision of one's transformed self. This section explores the essence of goal-setting:

Empowerment and Direction: Goals provide individuals with a sense of purpose and direction, weaving a tapestry of motivation that fuels their recovery journey.

Focus and Progress: By defining their aspirations, individuals channel their energy towards constructive pursuits, steering clear of old patterns. Goals serve as markers of progress, illuminating the distance traveled.

Crafting the Journey: Defining Short-Term Goals

In the journey of recovery, the first steps are often short ones—a series of milestones that pave the way for lasting change. This section guides readers through the process of crafting short-term goals:

Specific and Attainable: Short-term goals should be specific, achievable, and aligned with the broader vision of recovery. From reducing substance use to attending therapy sessions, these goals form the scaffolding of transformation.

Measurable and Time-Bound: Tangible progress lies in measurable goals with defined timelines. Readers are encouraged to set time-bound milestones that foster a sense of accomplishment.

From Seeds to Summits: Unveiling Long-Term Goals

While short-term goals lay the foundation, long-term goals cast a vision of lasting transformation. This section unveils the process of defining profound aspirations:

Dreams of Change: Long-term goals encompass a wide spectrum, from sustained sobriety to rebuilding relationships and pursuing passions. These goals embody the transformed self that readers envision.

Breakdown and Strategy: Transforming these aspirations into reality requires strategy. Readers are guided to break down long-term goals into manageable steps and strategies that cultivate steady progress.

The Symphony of Success: A Melody of Short-Term and Long-Term

In the heart of recovery, the harmonious interplay of short-term and long-term goals orchestrates success. This chapter concludes by emphasizing the need for balance—a symphony where daily victories align with the grand crescendo of ultimate transformation.

With the brush of goal-setting, readers paint their recovery journey—a canvas of purpose, milestones, and aspirations. It's a chapter that invites individuals to dream, plan, and journey towards the embodiment of their transformed selves. As the echoes of achievement resound, the power of setting recovery goals is revealed—a beacon that leads from addiction's shadows to the vibrant landscape of possibility.

CHAPTER 6

BUILDING A SUPPORTIVE NETWORK

"Networking is not about just connecting people. It's about connecting people with people, people with ideas, and people with opportunities."

- Michele Jennae

In the tapestry of addiction recovery, the threads of support weave a fabric of strength, resilience, and transformation. This chapter casts a spotlight on the invaluable role of friends, family, and support groups—the pillars that elevate individuals on their journey towards healing.

The Pillars of Strength: Allies in Recovery

As the recovery journey unfolds, the embrace of a supportive network serves as a steadfast anchor. This section explores the profound impact of allies:

Families as Foundations: Family members stand as pillars of unwavering support. Their empathy, understanding, and encouragement create a nurturing environment that fuels recovery.

Friends as Champions: Friends who rally around the journey offer a lifeline of companionship. Their presence and understanding light the way through dark times.

Support Groups as Sanctuaries: Support groups provide a haven of shared experiences. They connect individuals with peers who empathize, validate, and uplift, creating a tapestry of collective strength.

Crafting Conversations: Communicating with Loved Ones

Initiating conversations about addiction with loved ones can be a transformative step. This section offers guidance on effective communication:

Choose the Right Time and Place: Opt for a setting where all parties are comfortable and can engage without interruptions. Approach the conversation with a spirit of openness.

Speak from the Heart: Express your feelings, struggles, and aspirations with authenticity. Open communication fosters understanding and paves the way for support.

Educate and Embrace: Share information about addiction to dispel misconceptions and foster empathy. Embrace loved ones with the understanding that addiction is a complex challenge.

Inviting Allies into the Journey

Once the lines of communication are drawn, the next step is to invite loved ones into the recovery journey. This section unveils the art of requesting support:

Be Transparent: Clearly articulate your needs for support, whether it's through active listening, encouragement, or assistance in times of struggle.

Set Boundaries: While support is vital, establishing boundaries ensures that you maintain a balance between your journey and the needs of loved ones.

The Symphony of Healing: Allies Unite

In the symphony of recovery, the presence of friends, family, and support groups creates a harmonious melody of healing. Chapter 5 concludes with the reminder that building a supportive network is not just a solitary endeavor—it's a collaboration that enriches the recovery journey.

Through shared laughter, tears, and triumphs, allies stand as beacons, illuminating the path from darkness to light. The chapter celebrates the bonds forged on this journey—threads of connection that inspire, uplift, and remind individuals that they are never alone. As the symphony of healing resounds, the transformative power of a supportive network takes center stage—a resounding testament to the strength of unity in the tapestry of recovery.

CHAPTER 7

CREATING HEALTHY HABITS

"It is easier to prevent disease than to cure it."

- Benjamin Franklin

In the canvas of addiction recovery, the strokes of healthy habits paint a vibrant landscape of rejuvenation and well-being. This chapter delves into the transformative power of daily routines—fusing exercise, nutrition, and sleep—to pave the way for a life resplendent with vitality.

The Foundation of Wellness: Daily Routines

At the core of recovery lies the foundation of well-being—a daily routine that nourishes the body, mind, and spirit. This section delves into the significance of establishing healthy habits:

Harmony of Body and Mind: Healthy habits create a harmonious interplay between physical and mental well-being. Through deliberate choices, individuals cultivate an environment conducive to healing.

Empowerment through Routine: Daily routines empower individuals with a sense of control, fostering a structured framework that bolsters resilience and self-discipline.

The Elements of Transformation: Exercise, Nutrition, and Sleep

In the symphony of well-being, three elements—exercise, nutrition, and sleep—compose a melody of transformation. This section walks readers through each element:

Exercise as Empowerment: Incorporating exercise into daily routines infuses energy and vitality. Physical activity releases endorphins, alleviating stress and anxiety while fostering a sense of achievement.

Fueling Nourishment: Nutrition forms the cornerstone of vitality. Nourishing the body with wholesome foods provides the nutrients required for healing, rejuvenation, and mental clarity.

Restorative Sleep: Sleep is the canvas upon which the masterpiece of recovery is painted. Quality sleep rejuvenates the mind, strengthens immunity, and optimizes cognitive function—key components of the recovery journey.

The Ripple Effect: Positive Impact on Recovery

Healthy habits are not just individual pursuits; they have a profound impact on the trajectory of recovery. This section unveils the interconnected web of physical and mental well-being:

Balanced Mood and Emotions: A healthy lifestyle nurtures emotional resilience. Physical activity and proper nutrition contribute to stable moods, while adequate sleep enhances emotional equilibrium.

Stress Resilience: Healthy habits equip individuals with the tools to manage stress effectively. Regular exercise, a balanced diet, and sufficient sleep fortify the body's stress response.

Crafting a Transformational Routine

The art of establishing a transformative routine is multifaceted and unique to each individual. This section offers practical guidance:

Set Realistic Goals: Tailor your routine to your needs, setting achievable goals for exercise, nutrition, and sleep.

Start Small and Build: Begin with manageable steps and gradually build your routine. Small victories create a ripple effect of motivation.

Consistency and Adaptability: Consistency breeds success, but adaptability is equally crucial. Adjust your routine as circumstances change to maintain its relevance.

The Symphony of Well-Being: Daily Habits Unite

In the symphony of recovery, the harmonious interplay of daily habits creates a symphony of well-being. Chapter 6 concludes by emphasizing the transformative power of these habits—a daily dance that nurtures the body, mind, and spirit.

Through exercise, nutrition, and sleep, individuals compose a melody of vitality—a testament to their commitment to transformation. As the curtain rises on each day, the choice to embrace healthy habits becomes an anthem of renewal—a beacon that illuminates the path from addiction's shadows to the sunrise of wellness and thriving.

CHAPTER 8

COPING MECHANISMS AND STRESS MANAGEMENT

"In times of stress, the best thing we can do for each other is to listen with

> **our ears and our hearts and to be assured that our questions are just as important as our answers."**
>
> **- Fred Rogers**

In the labyrinth of recovery, the lanterns of coping mechanisms illuminate the path, guiding individuals through the challenges of stress, anxiety, and cravings. This chapter delves into the realm of resilience, unveiling an array of strategies—from mindfulness to creative expression—that empower individuals to navigate the currents of emotions and cravings with grace.

Navigating Storms: Coping Strategies for Resilience

When the tempest of stress, anxiety, and cravings brews, coping strategies serve as anchors of resilience. This section introduces the importance of cultivating effective coping mechanisms:

Empowerment through Choice: Coping mechanisms offer individuals the power of choice—a toolkit to manage emotions, mitigate triggers, and navigate the ebb and flow of recovery.

Stress as Catalyst: Stressors become catalysts for growth when met with adaptive coping strategies. These mechanisms reshape challenges into opportunities for personal transformation.

Mindful Presence: Embracing the Present Moment

Mindfulness stands as a cornerstone of emotional regulation. This section explores mindfulness techniques that foster present-moment awareness:

Breath as Anchor: Deep breathing exercises tether individuals to the present, anchoring them in the midst of turmoil. Controlled breath calms the nervous system, inviting a sense of tranquility.

Grounding in Senses: Mindful engagement with the senses—sight, sound, touch, taste, and smell—serves as a lifeline to the present moment, disconnecting individuals from the grip of past regrets and future anxieties.

Meditative Sojourn: Inner Retreat

Meditation invites individuals to journey within—a sanctuary of peace and clarity. This section unveils the transformative power of meditation:

Guided Imagery: Visualization techniques transport individuals to serene landscapes, easing the grip of cravings and cultivating a sense of calm.

Body Scan: Mindful body scans dissolve tension, harmonizing the mind-body connection and enabling individuals to listen to the wisdom of their bodies.

Creative Alchemy: Expressive Outlets

Creativity becomes a vessel of emotional expression, channeling emotions into artistic masterpieces. This section explores the art of creative outlets:

Artistic Expression: Drawing, painting, writing, and music offer a canvas for emotions. Creative outlets transform emotions into tangible creations, fostering healing and self-discovery.

Physical Release: Engaging in physical activities like dance or movement releases pent-up energy and emotions, offering an outlet for stress and cravings.

Crafting Your Toolbox: Personalizing Coping Strategies

Effective coping strategies are as unique as the individuals who embrace them. This section empowers readers to curate their personal toolbox of coping mechanisms:

Experiment and Discover: Explore different techniques to find those that resonate with you. Not all coping strategies work for everyone, so be open to experimentation.

Consistency and Adaptation: Consistency in practice deepens the impact of coping mechanisms. However, adaptability ensures that your toolbox evolves alongside your needs.

The Symphony of Resilience: Coping Strategies Converge

In the symphony of recovery, coping mechanisms harmonize with inner strength, guiding individuals through the tumultuous seas of emotions and cravings. Chapter 7 concludes with the reminder that coping is not about eradicating challenges, but about navigating them with grace and empowerment.

Through mindfulness, meditation, and creative expression, individuals unveil the art of emotional mastery—a testament to their capacity to transform adversity into growth. As the echoes of resilience resound, the transformative power of coping strategies takes center stage—an anthem of empowerment that leads from vulnerability to triumph in the symphony of recovery.

CHAPTER 9

BREAKING TRIGGERS AND PATTERNS

"The first step towards getting somewhere is to decide you're not going to stay where you are."

- J.P. Morgan

Within the tapestry of recovery, the art of breaking triggers and patterns emerges as a beacon of empowerment—a journey that unravels the threads of addiction's grip. This chapter delves into the intricate dance of self-awareness and transformation, guiding readers to identify triggers, navigate challenges, and craft new narratives of resilience.

Triggers Unveiled: Navigating the Maze

Triggers—those subtle cues that ignite the flame of addictive behavior—lie scattered across the landscape of daily life. This section sheds light on the importance of trigger identification:

Recognizing the Unseen: Triggers can be elusive, embedded in places, people, emotions, or even routine actions. Becoming attuned to these triggers is a profound step toward liberation.

Navigating Environments: Identifying triggering environments allows individuals to prepare themselves and create strategies for navigating challenges.

Strategies of Evasion: Navigating Triggers

Escaping the clutches of triggers requires a strategic approach. This section unveils strategies to evade and mitigate triggers:

Avoidance: When possible, avoiding triggering situations is an effective tactic. This could involve changing routines, limiting exposure, or crafting new environments.

Substitution: Replace negative habits with positive alternatives. For instance, if stress triggers cravings, adopt relaxation techniques or engage in physical activities to channel that energy.

Narratives of Empowerment: Rewriting Patterns

Patterns of behavior are etched in repetition, but they can be rewoven into narratives of empowerment. This section explores the art of pattern disruption:

Thought Rewiring: Challenge distorted thoughts that perpetuate negative patterns. Replace self-defeating beliefs with affirming, empowering ones.

Behavioral Interventions: Introduce intentional actions to break habitual cycles. Engage in activities that divert attention from triggers and infuse positivity.

A New Canvas: Embracing Change

Breaking triggers and patterns isn't just about erasing old habits—it's about creating a new canvas for growth. This section empowers readers to embark on this transformative journey:

Self-Compassion: Embrace imperfection with self-compassion. Understand that relapses are part of the process, but they don't define your journey.

Journaling and Reflection: Document your triggers, patterns, and progress. Journaling fosters self-awareness and serves as a compass for change.

The Symphony of Transformation: Unraveling and Reweaving

In the symphony of recovery, the journey of breaking triggers and patterns harmonizes with the orchestra of resilience. Chapter 8 concludes by reminding readers that the unraveling of triggers and patterns is an act of self-reclamation.

Through self-awareness, avoidance strategies, and pattern disruption, individuals don the mantle of transformation—a testament to their innate capacity to rewrite narratives and sculpt a life unbound by addiction's chains. As the echoes of empowerment resound, the transformative power of breaking triggers and patterns takes center stage—an anthem of liberation in the symphony of recovery.

CHAPTER 10

UNDERSTANDING RELAPSE AND RESILIENCE

"Resilience is knowing that you are the only one that has the power and the responsibility to pick yourself up."

- Mary Holloway

Within the journey of recovery, the path is not always linear; it meanders through peaks and valleys. This chapter unravels the intricate relationship between relapse and resilience—an exploration of setbacks that illuminate the path forward.

The Ebb and Flow: Relapse as a Teacher

Relapse, often seen as a shadow, is not the endpoint but a fork in the road—a moment of reflection and redirection. This section illuminates the concept of relapse:

Nature of Relapse: Relapses are not failures; they are part of the recovery journey. They offer insight into vulnerabilities and triggers, guiding individuals toward self-discovery.

Learning from Setbacks: Relapses hold lessons. By understanding the circumstances that led to a relapse, individuals can unearth valuable insights for future resilience.

The Armor of Resilience: Bouncing Back

Resilience emerges as the armor that transforms relapses into stepping stones. This section delves into the art of fortifying resilience:

Embracing Self-Compassion: In the aftermath of a relapse, self-compassion is essential. Rather than self-condemnation, practice self-kindness, recognizing that relapses are opportunities for growth.

Harnessing Support: Lean on your support network during challenging times. Friends, family, and support groups bolster resilience, offering guidance and encouragement.

Strategies of Transformation: Moving Forward

Resilience isn't merely a shield—it's a set of strategies that propel individuals forward. This section uncovers the strategies that transform relapses into catalysts for growth:

Reflect and Learn: Analyze the circumstances leading to a relapse. What were the triggers? What coping strategies faltered? Use this information to adapt your approach.

Develop Coping Skills: Strengthen your arsenal of coping mechanisms. Equip yourself with tools to navigate stress, cravings, and triggers effectively.

Writing Your Resilience Story: Turning the Page

Understanding relapse and resilience is about crafting a narrative that unfolds with courage. This section empowers readers to write their resilience stories:

Shifting Perspectives: Relapses are chapters, not the entire story. Embrace them as turning points that lead to deeper self-awareness and resilience.

Goal Reevaluation: Assess your recovery goals. Are they realistic? Adjust them if needed to set yourself up for success.

The Symphony of Transformation: Relapse and Resilience Dance

In the symphony of recovery, relapse and resilience dance in harmony—a duet of setbacks and triumphs. Chapter 9 concludes by illuminating that relapse is not a final note, but a note of renewal.

Through self-compassion, support, and strategic reflection, individuals harness the art of resilience—a testament to their ability to rise from the ashes of relapse. As the echoes of resilience resound, the transformative power of understanding relapse and resilience takes center stage—an anthem of growth in the symphony of recovery.

CHAPTER 11

EMBRACING NEW BEGINNINGS

"The beginning is the most important part of the work."

- Plato

In journey of recovery the final chapter unfurls as a celebration—a testament to the resilience that births new beginnings. As the journey of transformation culminates, this chapter illuminates the path to embracing a life unshackled by addiction—a life of sobriety, purpose, and personal growth.

The Metamorphosis of Self: A Journey Unveiled

Recovery is not just about quitting a substance or behavior; it's a profound metamorphosis of self. This section delves into the transformative power of the journey:

From Darkness to Light: The recovery journey is a passage from the shadows into the light. It's about shedding the weight of addiction and stepping into the brilliance of self-discovery.

Discovering Authenticity: Recovery unveils the authentic self-buried beneath the layers of addiction. Embrace this newfound authenticity—a gift that shines brightly.

The Tapestry of Sobriety: Navigating New Waters

Sobriety isn't merely the absence of addiction—it's a life brimming with possibilities. This section guides readers on navigating the waters of sobriety:

Celebrating Milestones: Mark your milestones, whether it's a day, a week, or a year of sobriety. Each step is a victory—a testament to your strength and growth.

Finding Joy in Everyday Life: Sobriety unveils a world of wonder that addiction often conceals. Embrace the beauty of life's simple moments, finding joy in the mundane.

The Garden of Personal Growth: Cultivating a Flourishing Life

Recovery isn't just about quitting—it's about blossoming. This section illuminates the garden of personal growth:

Pursuing Passions: Reclaim your passions and hobbies that may have taken a back seat during addiction. Engaging in activities you love enriches your journey.

Setting New Goals: As addiction fades, new aspirations emerge. Set goals that align with your values, propelling you toward a life of purpose and fulfillment.

Weaving the Tapestry of Tomorrow: Forward and Beyond

Embracing new beginnings is about looking forward with hope and determination. This section empowers readers to continue their journey beyond the final page:

Staying Mindful: Maintain mindfulness as you navigate life's challenges. Mindfulness anchors you in the present moment, fostering resilience.

Continuing Support: Lean on your support network even as you embrace new beginnings. Friends, family, and support groups are pillars of strength.

The Symphony of Transformation: A New Beginning's Overture

As this chapter draws to a close, the symphony of transformation crescendos with an overture of hope and renewal. Embracing new beginnings is about recognizing that the journey is ongoing—a continuous evolution toward a life of authenticity, sobriety, and personal growth.

Through the prism of recovery, the journey becomes a masterpiece—a symphony of resilience, transformation, and triumph. As the echoes of new beginnings resound, readers step into the spotlight of their own symphony—a testament to the beauty of embracing life's infinite possibilities.

CHAPTER 12

INSPIRING RECOVERY STORIES

"If you can quit for a day, you can quit for a lifetime."

- Benjamin Alire Saenz

In the mosaic of recovery, real-life stories become the vibrant tesserae that paint a portrait of hope, resilience, and triumph. This chapter is a tapestry woven with diverse threads—stories of individuals who defied the odds, battled their demons, and emerged victorious, lighting the path for others.

A Symphony of Transformation: Narratives of Triumph

Each recovery story is a symphony—an orchestration of struggle, perseverance, and transformation. This section showcases narratives that inspire:

From Despair to Hope: Meet Sarah, who battled the darkness of substance addiction. Through therapy, support groups, and sheer determination, she reclaimed her life and now works as a counselor, helping others navigate their journeys.

Rediscovering Purpose: Discover Mike's journey from the clutches of gambling addiction. His newfound passion for painting not only aided his recovery but ignited a creative fire that continues to illuminate his path.

United by Recovery: A Tapestry of Diversity

Recovery stories span across cultures, backgrounds, and challenges, united by the thread of courage. This section presents a mosaic of diverse experiences:

Breaking Chains of Stigma: Follow Maya's voyage—a tale of breaking free from the grip of opioid addiction. Her advocacy work empowers others to seek help without shame, fighting the stigma that often shrouds addiction.

Navigating Mental Health and Addiction: Meet Alex, whose battle with bipolar disorder intertwined with addiction. With professional help and unwavering determination, he now thrives, showcasing the symbiotic relationship between mental health and recovery.

Lessons of Triumph: Insights from the Journey

Addiction and recovery are complex and personal topics that affect many people in different ways. There is no one-size-fits-all solution or approach to overcoming addiction, but there are some common themes and strategies that can help. Here are some insights, stories, and practical advice related to addiction and recovery that I found from various sources:

- Insight: Addiction is not a moral failing or a lack of willpower, but a chronic brain disease that can be treated with professional help[1]. People who struggle with addiction often face stigma and discrimination, which can make them feel ashamed and isolated. However, there are many people who have recovered from addiction and are living fulfilling lives. Recovery is possible for anyone who seeks help and support.

- Story: Elizabeth Vargas, a former ABC television journalist, shared her story of addiction and recovery in her memoir

Between Breaths: A Memoir of Panic and Addiction[2]. She revealed how she hid her addiction and anxiety from the world for years, until she admitted that she was an alcoholic in 2014. She wrote about her journey of seeking treatment, attending Alcoholics Anonymous meetings, and finding hope and healing. She also spoke about the challenges and joys of being a mother, a wife, and a public figure while living in recovery.

- Advice: One of the most important steps in recovery is to find a supportive community of people who understand what you are going through and can offer you encouragement and guidance. You can join a peer support group, such as Alcoholics Anonymous or Narcotics Anonymous, where you can share your experiences, learn from others, and receive accountability. You can also reach out to your family and friends, or find a mentor or sponsor who can help you stay on track. Having a strong support system can make a huge difference in your recovery process.

- Insight: Recovery is not a linear or easy process, but a lifelong journey that requires constant effort and dedication. There will be ups and downs, successes and setbacks, temptations and triggers. However, you can learn from your mistakes and grow from your challenges. You can also celebrate your achievements and milestones, no matter how big or small. Recovery is not about being perfect, but about being honest, resilient, and hopeful.

- Story: Gina, a woman who started using heroin at the age of 13 and continued until she was 33, shared her story of addiction and recovery on the Recovery Centers of America blog[1]. She described how she fell 20 feet and broke her back and wrist while getting high, but still stayed out on the streets. She said that her family had to prepare her funeral, and that she told her mom that she was going to die from her disease. However, one day she had a moment of sanity and walked into a crisis center, asking for help. She went through detox, moved into a recovery house, started going to meetings, and found a group of women who loved her and supported her. She also reconnected with her family, who stood by her throughout her journey. She is now going to college to get her associate's degree in social work, and works in the recovery field.

- Advice: One of the most helpful tools in recovery is to find a healthy outlet for your emotions and creativity. You can engage in activities that bring you joy and satisfaction, such as hobbies, sports, arts, music, or volunteering. You can also express yourself through writing, journaling, meditation, or prayer. Finding a way to channel your energy and passion into something positive can help you cope with stress, boredom, loneliness, or anger. It can also help you discover new aspects of yourself and your potential.

Each story offers lessons that illuminate the path to recovery. This section distills these insights:

Resilience as the North Star: Through every story, resilience emerges as a guiding force—a testament to the human spirit's capacity to bounce back from adversity.

Support as a Beacon: The power of support—from friends, family, and fellow journeyers—shines as a beacon, dispelling isolation and kindling hope.

Your Symphony Awaits: Becoming Part of the Narrative

Inspiring recovery stories are not confined to pages; they unfold in the lives of readers. This section empowers readers to become the protagonists of their own stories:

Seeking Help: Reach out for help. Your journey begins with a single step—an act of courage that paves the way for transformation.

Writing Your Chapter: As you traverse the path of recovery, you become part of the symphony. Every choice, every triumph, adds a note to your unique narrative.

Numerous prominent individuals from around the globe

Numerous prominent individuals from around the globe have triumphed over their addictions, reshaping their lives in profound ways. Among them are celebrities who've candidly shared their recovery stories, kindling inspiration and encouraging others to seek help. Below are examples of such remarkable individuals:

- **Robert Downey Jr.**, renowned for his roles in blockbuster films like Iron Man and Avengers, struggled with drug use from an early age, affecting much of his early career. Battling high-profile arrests and addiction to alcohol, cocaine, and heroin, he underwent rehabilitation and emerged rehabilitated.

- **Angelina Jolie**, acclaimed actress and humanitarian, navigated an upbringing entwined with drug experimentation and mental health struggles. Overcoming cocaine, heroin, and other drugs, she prioritized personal growth, raising her children, and advocating for numerous causes.

- **Demi Lovato**, a singer and actress who rose to fame through Disney Channel, confronted alcohol and drug addiction while grappling with bipolar disorder and eating disorders. Her recovery journey, courageously shared through interviews and music, continues to inspire countless individuals.

- **Ngozi Okonjo-Iweala**, Nigerian economist and politician, battled corruption, poverty, cancer, and alcoholism in her unwavering quest to uplift her country. Overcoming addiction with the support of her family and faith, she serves as the director-general of the World Trade Organization.

- **Adeola Fayehun**, a Nigerian journalist and comedian renowned for her show "Keeping It Real With Adeola," humorously unveils societal and political issues while sharing her personal triumph over drug addiction. Her journey of recovery, fueled by journalism and faith, is a testament to her resilience.

- **Babatunde Olatunji**, a Nigerian musician who introduced African rhythms to the West, grappled with heroin addiction during his time in New York. His transformative experience led to quitting heroin, and he dedicated his life to promoting African culture and music.

These stories illuminate the power of determination, resilience, and the potential for transformation when battling addiction. Through their narratives, these individuals demonstrate that recovery is possible, providing hope and inspiration to those on their own journeys to healing.

The Symphony Continues: A Harmonious Future

As this chapter draws to a close, the echoes of inspiring recovery stories resound—an anthem of hope and possibility. Each story is a testament to the symphony of transformation, a source of inspiration for those seeking their own crescendo of triumph.

In the tapestry of recovery, stories converge, harmonizing into a melody that uplifts, motivates, and encourages. As readers reflect on these tales of triumph, they stand at the precipice of their own symphony—a journey imbued with strength, resilience, and the unwavering promise of renewal.

CHAPTER 13

RESOURCES AND NEXT STEP

In the symphony of recovery, this final chapter serves as a guidepost—a wellspring of resources and a compass pointing toward continued growth. As you navigate your journey, remember that you're never alone—countless resources, organizations, and helplines are here to accompany you.

A Tapestry of Support: Resources for Recovery

This section presents an array of resources, offering a lifeline of guidance and support:

Helplines: National helplines offer confidential assistance, providing a listening ear and expert advice.

- National Helpline for Substance Abuse and Mental Health: 1-800-662-HELP (4357)

- Alcoholics Anonymous (AA) Helpline: Check your local AA website for contact information

Websites and Online Communities: Online platforms offer valuable information, forums for sharing, and resources:

- Substance Abuse and Mental Health Services Administration (SAMHSA): www.samhsa.gov

- SMART Recovery: www.smartrecovery.org

- Reddit's Addiction and Recovery Subreddits: www.reddit.com/r/addiction, www.reddit.com/r/REDDITORSINRECOVERY

Sustaining Progress: Your Next Steps

This section provides guidance on maintaining momentum and progress:

Staying Accountable: Regular check-ins with a counselor, support group, or sponsor can help you stay on course and remain accountable.

Engaging in Self-Care: Prioritize self-care practices that nourish your mind, body, and soul—whether it's meditation, exercise, or pursuing hobbies.

Your Symphony of Renewal: Continuation of the Journey

As this chapter draws to a close, remember that recovery is a journey—an ongoing symphony of renewal. Each resource, each connection, fuels your progression:

Embracing Lifelong Learning: Continue to educate yourself about addiction, mental health, and coping strategies. Knowledge empowers.

Contributing to Others: Consider becoming a beacon of hope for someone else's journey. Share your experiences, lend a supportive hand, and foster a community of growth.

A Harmonious Overture: The Road Ahead

As the final notes of this chapter sound, let them reverberate—a harmonious overture to the road ahead.

Recovery is a tapestry woven with your courage, your choices, and your triumphs.

In the tapestry of recovery, resources are the stars that illuminate the night sky—guiding you toward continued transformation. As you venture forth, embrace the endless possibilities, maintain your resilience, and step confidently into the symphony of renewal that is your life.

Conclusion: A Symphony of Renewal

In the pages of this book, you've embarked on a journey—a symphony of renewal—a journey that echoes with stories of triumph, lessons of resilience, and the enduring melody of hope. As we bring this composition to a close, let's harmonize the key takeaways that resonate from each chapter:

Acceptance and Self-Reflection: Acknowledge your addiction with compassion, letting go of blame. Through self-reflection, uncover the patterns and triggers that led you here.

Seeking Professional Help: Reach out to healthcare professionals, therapists, and counselors. Their guidance will light your way through the labyrinth of recovery.

Setting Recovery Goals: Set clear, achievable goals—both short-term and long-term—unveiling a path toward your transformed future.

Building a Supportive Network: Engage your circle of loved ones and support groups. Communication and connection will be the bedrock of your journey.

Creating Healthy Habits: Embrace a healthy lifestyle—exercise, nutrition, and sleep. These habits will nurture your body and mind, fostering a strong foundation for recovery.

Coping Mechanisms and Stress Management: Equip yourself with an arsenal of coping strategies—mindfulness, meditation, and creativity—to navigate stress, anxiety, and cravings.

Breaking Triggers and Patterns: Identify triggers and rewrite your story. Replace negative habits with positive alternatives, stepping out of old patterns.

Understanding Relapse and Resilience: Understand that relapses are part of the journey. Learn from them, cultivate resilience, and continue moving forward.

Embracing New Beginnings: Embrace your transformation. Sobriety is a canvas, and your life—now free from addiction—holds infinite hues waiting to be explored.

Inspiring Recovery Stories: Draw strength from the stories of others who've walked this path. Their triumphs are a testament to the possibility of renewal.

Resources and Next Steps: Utilize resources and organizations to maintain your progress. Continue seeking help and stay committed to your journey.

A Final Note: Hope, Resilience, and Your Melody of Renewal

As you close this chapter and step into your tomorrow, remember this: you are not defined by your past, but by the courage and resilience you've displayed on your path to recovery. The symphony of renewal is your composition—a melody that resonates with the potential of a brighter future.

Your journey continues, not with the shackles of addiction, but with wings of transformation. Embrace each note, each choice, and each day as a harmonious affirmation of your renewal. The crescendo of your life's symphony awaits—a symphony of hope, resilience, and the promise of a brighter, uncharted horizon.

A systematic review conducted in 2014 highlighted that the observed prevalence rates of sexual addiction or hypersexual disorder span a range of 3% to 6% globally[3]. Research indicates that a significant majority of individuals dealing with sex addiction are male, constituting about 80%[3]. The phenomenon of hypersexuality affects approximately 3% to 10% of the general U.S. population, with a higher incidence among men than women. For every two to five males with hypersexuality, one woman experiences it. It's noteworthy that sexual addiction tends to take root around the age of 18, and individuals typically seek professional assistance around the age of 37[2].

REFERENCE

(1) Alcohol, Drugs and Addictive Behaviours - World Health Organization (WHO).
https://www.who.int/teams/mental-health-and-substance-use/alcohol-drugs-and-addictive-behaviours/drugs-psychoactive/cannabis.

(2) Global drug use - Statistics & Facts | Statista.

https://www.statista.com/topics/7786/gl
obal-drug-use/.

(3) World Drug Report 2021_Annex -
United Nations Office on Drugs and
Crime.
https://www.unodc.org/unodc/en/data-
and-analysis/wdr2021_annex.html.

(4) World Drug Report 2019: 35 million
people worldwide suffer from drug ....
https://www.unodc.org/unodc/en/frontpag
e/2019/June/world-drug-report-2019_-35-
million-people-worldwide-suffer-from-
drug-use-disorders-while-only-1-in-7-
people-receive-treatment.html.

(5) Harmful use of alcohol kills more
than 3 million people each year,
most....
https://www.who.int/news/item/21-09-
2018-harmful-use-of-alcohol-kills-more-
than-3-million-people-each-year--most-
of-them-men.

(6)
https://my.clevelandclinic.org/health/d
iseases/6407-addiction

(7) Types of Addiction and How They're Treated   -   Healthline. https://www.healthline.com/health/types -of-addiction.

(8) Types of Addiction: List of Addictions | HealthyPlace. https://www.healthyplace.com/addictions /addictions-information/types-of- addiction-list-of-addictions.

(9) Addiction: What It Is, Causes, Symptoms, Types & Treatment. https://my.clevelandclinic.org/health/d iseases/6407-addiction.

(10) Addiction: what is it? - NHS. https://www.nhs.uk/live-well/addiction- support/addiction-what-is-it/.

(11) 11 Powerful Recovery and Sobriety Memoirs to Inspire You | SELF. https://www.self.com/gallery/recovery- sobriety-memoirs.

(12) Drug Addiction Recovery Stories: Inspiring Accounts of Triumph and .... https://lantanarecovery.com/drug- addiction-recovery-stories-inspiring-

accounts-of-triumph-and-
transformation/.

(13) Personal Stories - Sober Recovery.
https://www.soberrecovery.com/recovery/
category/personal-stories/.

(14) True Stories of Addiction:
Educating and Inspiring.
https://detoxtorehab.com/true-stories-
of-addiction/true-stories-of-addiction-
educating-and-inspiring.

(15) 14 Celebrities in Recovery: Famous
Faces Who've Battled Addiction - WebMD.
https://www.webmd.com/mental-
health/addiction/ss/slideshow-celebs-
addiction-recovery.

(16) Celebrities Who Overcame
Addiction: 15 Recovery Stories -
Horizon Clinics.
https://horizonclinics.org/celebrities-
who-overcame-addiction/.

(17) 11 People Who Beat Addiction And
Changed Their Life Completely.
https://www.powerofpositivity.com/12-
people-who-beat-addiction-and-changed-
their-life-completely/.

(18) 23 Famous Drug Addicts | Celebrity Substance Abuse & Addiction - AspenRidge. https://www.aspenridgerecoverycenters.com/celebrity-substance-abuse/.

(19) World Drug Report 2019: 35 million people worldwide suffer from drug .... https://www.unodc.org/unodc/en/frontpage/2019/June/world-drug-report-2019_-35-million-people-worldwide-suffer-from-drug-use-disorders-while-only-1-in-7-people-receive-treatment.html.

(20) Age Group Differences in Progress toward Reducing Substance Use ... - ASPE. https://aspe.hhs.gov/reports/age-group-differences-progress-toward-reducing-substance-use-disorders-2015-2018-issue-brief.

(21) Correlation Between Age and Addiction | Addiction Recovery. https://www.midwestdetoxcenter.com/rehab-blog/correlation-between-age-and-addiction/.

(22) Drug Addiction and Rehabilitation in Nigeria - Global Journals. https://globaljournals.org/GJMR_Volume1

2/6-Drug-Addiction-and-Rehabilitation-
in-Nigeria.pdf.

(23)   The   Problem   Of   Drugs/Substance
Abuse In Nigeria: A Symposium By ....
https://www.nafdac.gov.ng/the-problem-
of-drugs-substance-abuse-in-nigeria-a-
symposium-by-professor-mojisola-
christianah-adeyeye-director-general-
nafdac-at-the-university-of-benin-
benin-city/.

(24) 15 Of The Best Nigerian Books -
BOOK   RIOT.   https://bookriot.com/best-
nigerian-books/.

(25) 19 Books About Addiction: Helpful
Resources   for   Recovery   -   Choosing
Therapy.
https://www.choosingtherapy.com/addicti
on-books/.

(26) 25 Powerful Books About Nigeria &
Nigerian   Culture.
https://www.theuncorkedlibrarian.com/bo
oks-about-nigeria/.

(27)http://creativecommons.org/licenses
/by-nc/3.0/%29.

(26) Living Recovery: True Stories of Addiction Recovery. https://recoverycentersofamerica.com/blogs/living-recovery-true-stories-of-addiction-recovery/.

(29) 11 Powerful Recovery and Sobriety Memoirs to Inspire You | SELF. https://www.self.com/gallery/recovery-sobriety-memoirs.

(30) Share Your Story | SAMHSA. https://www.samhsa.gov/brss-tacs/recovery-support-tools/share-your-story.

(31) Recovery Stories | Breaking the Chains of Addiction - DrugRehab.com. https://www.drugrehab.com/stories-of-recovery/.

(32) Sexual addiction - Wikipedia. https://en.wikipedia.org/wiki/Sexual_addiction.

(33) Sex Addiction, Hypersexuality and Compulsive Sexual Behavior. https://my.clevelandclinic.org/health/treatments/22690-sex-addiction-hypersexuality-and-compulsive-sexual-behavior.

(34) Sexual health - World Health Organization (WHO). https://www.who.int/health-topics/sexual-health.

(35) The prevalence rate of sexual violence worldwide: a trend analysis .... https://bmcpublichealth.biomedcentral.com/articles/10.1186/s12889-020-09926-5.

ABOUT THE AUTHOR

Evaristus Chukwugoziem Okonkwo's life journey began in the vibrant town of Nnewi in the Nnewi North Local Government Area of Anambra State, Nigeria. Born on the 10th of March, 1988, he brought with him a spirit of curiosity and determination that would shape his path in the years to come.

His educational voyage was a tapestry woven with diverse experiences. It commenced at Choice Nursery and Primary School, where the seeds of knowledge were sown. This foundation led him to Akamili Central School (Hill), continuing his educational ascent. Thriving on the thirst for learning, he embarked on a new chapter at Marist Comprehensive College Nteje, where his intellectual horizons expanded.

Evaristus's quest for knowledge knew no bounds, as evidenced by his pursuit of education at Summit International

School. However, it was Abia State University Uturu that provided him with a profound academic home. Majoring in Environmental Resource Management, he delved into the intricacies of environmental stewardship—a theme that would resonate throughout his career.

His academic endeavors acted as a stepping stone to a career woven with diversity. The corridors of Airtel Nigeria welcomed him, exposing him to the dynamic world of telecommunications. The bustling environment of Mobil Service Station taught him valuable lessons in customer service and operational excellence. Amidst the vibrant landscapes of Cway Nigeria, he contributed to the realms of marketing and distribution.

In the present, Evaristus has found his purpose within the Anambra State Ministry of Environment, where he serves as the Onitsha Zonal Forest Officer. This role embodies his commitment to environmental conservation—a testament to his dedication, resilience, and a profound connection to his community.

Beyond his professional endeavours, Evaristus Chukwugoziem Okonkwo is defined by his devotion to family. His life partner, Mrs. Chinenye Juliet Okonkwo, shares in his dreams, supporting him through every endeavour. Together, they have been blessed with the joy of parenthood, nurturing their children and imparting values that enrich their lives.

Evaristus's journey embodies his role as a seeker of knowledge, a guardian of the environment, and a proud contributor to his community. With each step, he embraces the lessons of the past while forging ahead with aspirations for the future. His voyage is one of inspiration—a testament to the transformative power of determination, unity, and an unyielding commitment to growth.

www.ingramcontent.com/pod-product-compliance
Lightning Source LLC
Chambersburg PA
CBHW050924260726

48660CB00001B/393